D1095904

Cosmic Grooves:

Sagittarius

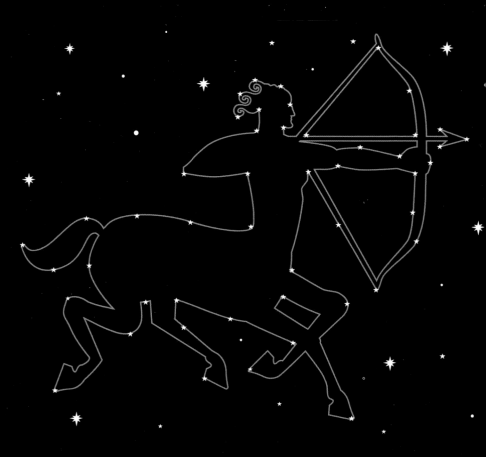

Cosmic Grooves:

Sagittarius

by Jane Hodges

CHRONICLE BOOKS
SAN FRANCISCO

RHINO

Sagittarius

November 23 to December 21

Element: *Fire*

Quality: *Mutable, a sign that adapts*

Motto: *"I seek"*

Planetary Ruler: ♃ *Jupiter, the planet of fortune and public life*

Jupiter's Influence: *Sagittarians are adventurers who perceive new opportunities around every corner. Driven by a natural love of learning, they prefer immersion and experience to abstract study. The Sagittarian pursuit of adventure and stimulation means these people frequently change plans to accommodate new agendas, so this sign can have trouble with long-term commitments. This can irritate those who depend on them, but friendly Sagittarians are hard to resent, and they themselves move past such conflicts easily.*

Symbol: *The Archer*

Archer's Influence: *Sporty Sagittarians hunt literally and figuratively for new knowledge and experience to expand their perspective. These direct and fearless individuals enjoy the adventure of discovering where their intellectual "arrows" will take them. This sign prizes honesty. Although at times Sagittarians can be blunt and tactless in their quest for the truth, their fiery spirit makes them fun companions. Their interest in the outdoors, athletics, and travel often has a spiritual dimension.*

How to recognize a Sagittarius:
Long legs, enthusiastic storytelling, sporty outfit
Pick-up line: *"If you could travel anywhere,
where would you go?"*
What a Sagittarius wants: *Freedom, experience*
What a Sagittarius needs: *Discipline, education*
Jukebox selection: *"Don't Worry,
Be Happy"*

Sagittarians are the zodiac's philosophers and gypsies. Ruled by expansive Jupiter ♃, people born under this experimental sign thrive on travel and adventure—activities that allow them to test their theories and expand their ideas about the world. In accordance with their fire sign, Sagittarians are impulsive, optimistic, and idealistic. They strive to be totally honest, but often put their foot in their mouth as they tactlessly deliver their opinion. Driven by a need for experience, they may burn through money in an attempt to see and do and try everything around them. Sagittarius is also, interestingly, one of the least materialistic signs, and Sagittarians prefer accumulating wisdom to money. Hungry for life experience and to expand their own philosophies, they can be the ambitious solo scholar who spends nights in the lab or the party animal who burns the candle on both ends.

Children of this sign will love nature, and many have impressive coordination or athletic skills for their age. They gravitate toward a very active lifestyle, and many pursue intense sports that demand dedication and training, such as gymnastics or horseback riding.

Outgoing Sagittarius teens will be flirty and, though they may appear straight-laced, often find shortcuts to help them hurry through school. They learn by doing—taking field trips, doing internships, mentoring—rather than by intensive study or heavy reading. They thrive on trips, so car access is a must. In adulthood, Sagittarians retain a youthful spirit of adventure and will create a flexible schedule that allows time for exploring.

Sagittarians find pleasure in seeing new places. They'll go shopping in out-of-the-way neighborhoods just to visit them and line up first at any swanky new restaurant to examine which paparazzi appeared. They will often bring pets with them, since Sagittarians love taking care of animals. If they can't hit the road literally, they'll travel imaginatively by participating in theater or Web surfing, or undertake spiritual exploration on their own. Because they are opinionated and good at motivating others, Sagittarians will get friends involved, whether it's to go see a local band, run in a charity race, or do political volunteer work. They're not interested in bureaucracy and adore spontaneous activities. Life, for this sign, is a philosophical quest that demands travel and examination.

Sporty Sagittarians like world beats and party tunes. These folks choose music that encourages social, creative, and intellectual freedom.

Optimistic — Sagittarians see no need to look at the negative side of life. The sunny, lighthearted spirit that gives them so much magnetism is celebrated in *Don't Worry, Be Happy* by Bobby McFerrin.

Inspiring — When Archers are enthusiastic about something, they can rally the masses to join a cause, and *I'm So Excited* by the Pointer Sisters captures their fiery energy.

Wild — Without some structure, Sagittarian impulses can make Archer folks scattered and unpredictable. Their creative urge is described in *All Fired Up* by Pat Benatar.

Liberated — More than other signs, self-motivated Sagittarians avoid the shackles of 9-to-5 jobs, debt, and societal expectations, which is what *All Right Now* by Free is all about.

Leisurely — *Ramblin' Man* by The Allman Brothers Band must be about a Sagittarius, because this experimental sign loves to travel far and wide, wandering in and out of others' lives.

Courageous — Fiery Archers aren't afraid to fight or speak out for what they believe in, and *One Tin Soldier* performed by Coven

notes their tendency to be blunt about their feelings in
any conflict.

Freedom-loving	This sign is more interested in exploration than making a nest egg, and The Guess Who's version of *Share the Land* shows that property and privacy are the furthest thing from communal Sagittarians' minds.
Adventurous	Spontaneous Archers will go anywhere at the last minute. The way they relish diving into the unexpected gets a nod of respect in *Last Train to Clarksville* performed by The Monkees.
Cheerful	For an open-minded Sagittarian, life is full of inspiring challenges rather than setbacks, so *The Happy Song* by Otis Redding is an appropriate anthem for this sign.
Accepting	Archers have an unfailing belief in the power of positive thought and *Everyday* sung by Buddy Holly acknowledges this knack for looking on the sunny side of life.
Virtuous	Archers won't even tell white lies. *Truth and Honesty* sung by Aretha Franklin could be this sign's theme song.
Expansive	From gypsy to intellectual, from philosopher to vagabond, the archetypes of the Sagittarian persona are mythologized in *Sagittarius* by Cannonball Adderley.

Born under a fire sign, Sagittarians are enthusiastic and inspired. They see work as a kind of sport, filled with drama and adrenaline-pumping decision-making that's all in good fun. Competition invigorates them, and their optimistic belief in their success potential gives them the power to rally others. Sagittarians dislike being tied down in the office and sitting through long meetings, and while adept at office politics, prefer to use their charm to negotiate a position that affords them freedom. Whether this means an expense account to wine and dine clients, an unconventional work week, or an assignment in the far-flung field office, Sagittarians need flexibility. They will hold many jobs—or many job roles within one company—during their career, for each new experience whets their appetite for the work that lies around the bend. Since Sagittarians aren't content to hear what happens in a different field, they may change careers to experience other jobs for themselves. This trait, when it stems from commitment phobia, can give them a lack of depth, but more frequently their penchant for change gives them added insight.

Sagittarius Careers

Sociable Sagittarians deal well both with the public and with office politics. They are excellent trend-spotters and take an experimental approach in anything they do. Those who work in business often find success in entertainment, as Sagittarian Charles Ringling did when he founded his famous circus. The fast pace of Hollywood and filmmaking, where Sagittarian Steven Spielberg made a name for himself, appeals to this sociable sign. Whether a Sagittarian is a pro athlete like Boris Becker, a martial arts master like Bruce Lee, or a sports promoter like Don King, those born under this sign can often enjoy a successful sports career. Philosophical Sagittarians also make good teachers at all levels. They love any environment where they are paid to encourage new ideas and stoke debates. Travel-related positions in advertising, sales, diplomacy, or journalism satisfy Sagittarian wanderlust and provide enough variety to keep them from getting bored, as do positions in business and banking that deal with foreign trade or currency. Many Archers also make a living from their love of animals and nature by working as veterinarians or forest rangers.

Sagittarians value friendship and variety in a relationship over routine and domesticity. Both men and women born under the sign of the Archer will forgive many foibles in a mate as long as their partner is honest, open-minded, and flexible. Philosophical Sagittarians are on a quest for experience and don't want—and won't offer—a life of material comfort. Their idea of security is maintaining a steady stream of connections, passions, and hobbies that take them to new worlds and new ways of living life. They're always on the move, and their ideal mate will allow them the freedom to change careers, passions, and destinations—and support them when they do so. While Sagittarians begin many projects enthusiastically, their tendency to change midstream will need to be checked—gently—by a more consistent partner. These people love sharing sports, travel, and adventure with a loved one.

Sagittarius Relationships

Sagittarius & Aries (*March 21 to April 20*)	Passionate
Sagittarius & Taurus (*April 21 to May 21*)	Harmonious
Sagittarius & Gemini (*May 22 to June 21*)	Passionate
Sagittarius & Cancer (*June 22 to July 22*)	Challenging
Sagittarius & Leo (*July 23 to August 23*)	Passionate
Sagittarius & Virgo (*August 24 to September 22*)	Challenging
Sagittarius & Libra (*September 23 to October 23*)	Passionate
Sagittarius & Scorpio (*October 24 to November 22*)	Harmonious
Sagittarius & Sagittarius (*November 23 to December 21*)	Harmonious
Sagittarius & Capricorn (*December 22 to January 20*)	Harmonious
Sagittarius & Aquarius (*January 21 to February 20*)	Passionate
Sagittarius & Pisces (*February 21 to March 20*)	Challenging

Miss Sagittarius and Her Men

The Archer woman can be friendly and funny, like
Sagittarians Lucy Liu and Julianne Moore, or an athletic
siren, like Jupiter-ruled Kim Basinger and
Darryl Hannah. Regardless of her demeanor, this optimistic
woman wants a mate who's a friend as well as
a lover and who won't squelch her adventurous spirit.
He'll have to be practical enough to ground her, yet believe in
her enough to give her the freedom she needs.

Sagittarius Woman & Aries Man

Amy Grant seeks Vince Gill.

She likes the way this aggressive, cheerful man knows what he wants and goes after it. For this duo to work, though, Mr. Aries will have to realize that he can't always come first. Though she is a tomboy at times, passionate Miss Sagittarius is also a bit of a princess and enjoys being pursued. Fortunately, this man loves a challenge and finds this adventurous lady well worth chasing. In bed, this sporty pair will have a great time—his open-minded attitude blends well with her bold, experimental approach to sex. She gets a kick out of his demanding nature and appreciates the way he anchors the relationship. He enjoys the fact that, for once, he's met a woman who's not only twice as gutsy as he is, but also capable of making him grow. Miss Sagittarius might even get Mr. Aries to take up a good cause or two. Together, they'll share a life of adventures and travel.

Sagittarius Woman & Taurus Man

Connie Francis seeks Roy Orbison.

Plucky Miss Sagittarius finds rooted Mr. Taurus funny and sexy, and since he's similarly attracted to her it looks like a good match. However, if she wants an adventurous companion, she'll have to turn off the TV and ply him out from under the remote, because he is content with domesticity. Fortunately, she has a better chance of successfully getting him out of the house than other women do. He's tickled by her sassy outlook and impressed at the fast pace she keeps—he secretly knows he needs to change his curmudgeonly ways. His jealousy is touching to Miss Sagittarius, who is a constant but harmless flirt. In the bedroom, their dynamic works well, as her athleticism and his sensual stamina are well suited. He'll try to bring structure and security to her life—maybe by proposing that she move in—while she'll try to bring spontaneity and a sense of adventure to his. To make things last, they'll have to find a compromise between their conflicting natures. Harmony is possible if they can take turns letting common sense and freedom rule their decision-making.

Sagittarius Woman & Gemini Man

Sheila E. seeks Prince.

Sparks fly when these two adventurers meet. He's full of great ideas, and she's full of energy and pluck. If life is a journey, he's the well-read tour guide and she's the spontaneous backpacker. Given their independent, mutable signs, Miss Sagittarius is married only to her freedom, and Mr. Gemini is married only to his mind. Her desire to explore the physical world and his desire to make verbal sense of it make them excellent company. He can help her be more thoughtful of life's subtle details, while she can draw him out of his daydreams and into the real world, leading him places that fire up his experimental nature. This synergy carries over in their sex life—her daring approach, paired with his creative ideas, makes them extremely compatible in the bedroom. They may decide, after a short time, to tie the knot and head off on an adventurous honeymoon that lasts a lifetime.

Sagittarius Woman & Cancer Man

Christina Aguilera seeks Mick Fleetwood.

When the zodiac's Goddess of the Hunt meets the sensitive New Age Crab man, the result is a caring, imaginative duo. They both draw inspiration from their surroundings, but their ideal surroundings differ. Domestic Mr. Cancer realizes that this wandering woman needs someone stable and nurturing in her life—and that only true love will keep her in one place. He'll teach Miss Sagittarius that adventure doesn't always involve travel, and convince her that exploring their affections in private together is ultimately more rewarding than exploring the world alone. For her part, she'll teach him that leaving home redefines it. Sexually, he's old-fashioned, but as they grow familiar with one another he'll happily experiment to provide the spice she requires. Together, they can build a solid bridge between their two different worlds. It won't be easy to construct—and may be easier for her to cross than for him—but when complete it will be beautiful, and not at all what either of them expected.

Sagittarius Woman & Leo Man

Etta Jones seeks Isaac Hayes.

Both friendly and popular, these two make a fabulous couple. The Lion guy will do more than match her fast pace—he'll make their outings all the more fun by insisting they go *in style*. With Mr. Leo on hand to lavish Miss Sagittarius with praise and encouragement, her sporty optimism will become assured self-confidence. He teaches her to express her individuality more fully and to see herself as an accomplished superstar, rather than a student still in the throes of a course in life-long learning. She teaches him to let go of his need for an audience—to live in the moment—and meditate less on his exalted place in the world and more on the world itself. In bed, his penchant for drama and her energy and enthusiasm lead to fireworks. Mr. Leo is one of the few men who can get rambling Miss Sagittarius to unpack her bags and curl up by a roaring fire long enough to fall in love. They'll be friends as well as lovers, for this love match is made in the stars.

Sagittarius Woman & Virgo Man

Stacy Lattisaw seeks Freddie Mercury.

When Miss Sagittarius, the zodiac's sexiest explorer, meets this discriminating and tasteful man, she'll recognize their shared love of learning. On closer examination, however, they may realize that they're both looking for different things from their life's education. Earnest Mr. Virgo wants to learn from others' successes and mistakes and work toward perfection, while pioneering Miss Sagittarius wants to take off and explore uncharted waters. He wants to refine existing knowledge, while she wants to discover new ideas. Because they're both blunt, their differences come out in the open quickly. His judgments threaten to squelch her spontaneity, and he may not appreciate the way she laughs off his advice. He finds her sexy, but his gentlemanly affection isn't a natural match for her fiery, demanding style. She finds his restrained sexiness exciting, but ultimately not satisfying. Long-distance, this relationship could work for a time—after all, they're both independent thinkers who change their priorities frequently—but for lasting commitment, the learning curve may be too steep.

Sagittarius Woman & Libra Man

Edith Piaf seeks Bruce Springsteen.

Sweet-natured Mr. Libra provides the romance in this relationship, and gutsy Miss Sagittarius is happy to provide the variety. He loves her sporty optimism—the way she'll drop everything for a road trip, always be the life of the party, and disregard what others think of her. She finds this polite man sexy and endearing, and is charmed by the way he manages to organize groups—something she isn't patient enough to do. Together they make a popular, sought-out couple. He can help her curb her blunt tongue and learn to plan ahead, and she can teach him that he doesn't have to please everyone all the time. While she loves to get outdoors or pursue spiritual ideas, and he prefers to gallery-hop or socialize, they instinctively know how to split their time between these two worlds. In bed, her athleticism paired with his romanticism produces unforgettable fireworks. The result is a balanced, inspired relationship with long-lasting potential.

Sagittarius Woman & Scorpio Man

Tina Turner seeks Ike Turner.

These two charismatic folks share a deep commitment to personal growth. How they define that growth, though, differs greatly. Volatile Mr. Scorpio's emotions are greatly affected by his environment, while casual Miss Sagittarius handles life's ups and downs with philosophical detachment. If they commit, they can learn a lot from one another, for he excels at deep one-on-one connections while she pursues and navigates public life easily. She's unintimidated by his intensity, which leads to a good sexual match, but ultimately he may find her casual detachment unfulfilling. She'll try to laugh off his dark moods—a bad idea, since he wants a partner who respects the profundity he experiences in life—and may begin to resent how his attitude darkens her optimism. In her opinion, he would enjoy life more if he borrowed a little bit of her levity. These two are likely to part, but if they're brave enough to stay together, the necessary compromises could make them better people. Together, this intense duo can learn more about the world—and themselves—than they can on their own.

Sagittarius Woman & Sagittarius Man

June Pointer seeks Gregg Allman.

Two Sagittarians will form a solid friendship if they stay in one place long enough for it to develop. Once any kind of connection comes to life for them, it can't help but grow into romance. She loves the way this guy plans a thrilling road trip, and he loves the way she tells him to drive faster. He encourages her creativity, while she encourages him to take risks. Now and then they'll snap at each other—usually when they've overextended themselves with too many late nights of fun and too few hours of sleep—but this blunt duo forgives and forgets easily. Sexually, they share a similar athletic approach that is comfortable for both of them, but they will have to experiment to keep the variety alive. While this pair is friendly and sociable, the more time they spend together, the less time they may make for others, as they don't like the way a constant crowd cramps their style. They'll have to remind themselves that other people help spice up the evening rather than reduce its possibilities. They'll never lack for great company, since everyone wants to be around this dynamic duo.

Sagittarius Woman & Capricorn Man

Bette Midler seeks Robert Palmer.

Miss Sagittarius and Mr. Capricorn will befriend one another because they are both very honest people with high moral values concerning friendship. However, when things veer away from the platonic—which they most likely will, since he is sexy as well as charmingly earnest—the going gets tougher. As a couple, they deal with change differently. When it comes time to revise plans, which inevitably happens with the Archer woman, the straight-shooting Goat guy views her tendency to shift focus frustrating. She doesn't quite respect his traditional goals and finds his work ethic a bit staid. He's open to traveling with her, but only if he can pack his business cards, and this approach means he may not get to see much of his passport-toting woman. To make this relationship work, they should move in together and make time for their great athletic sex life, which is one of the most compatible areas of their shared existence. They know how to give each other freedom, so if they choose to commit, this relationship could be a long and happy one.

Sagittarius Woman & Aquarius Man

Britney Spears seeks Rick James.

It will take a long time for these two to meet since they're both constantly surrounded by friends, but the minute they start talking they'll feel like they've found a soulmate. Mr. Aquarius is a great match for Miss Sagittarius: he's good-looking, friendly, open-minded, and could care less about the conventions that hold back other men. If she can stop laughing at his jokes long enough to boldly kiss him, he'll be delighted. Together they will be the life of any party and the galvanizers of every cause. This thoughtful man can help her work on follow-through, reminding her that others count on her. Where he lacks focus, she has the drive to put him firmly back on course. This unconventional pair makes up their own rules as they go along. In bed, energetic Miss Sagittarius and erotic Mr. Aquarius know how to have a great time. They're the most sociable couple in town, and when they decide to tie the knot, the wedding will be as wild—and as endearingly eccentric—as the rest of their life to come.

Sagittarius Woman & Pisces Man

Sinead O'Connor seeks James Taylor.

This duo shares an interest in religion and mysticism that can either bind or separate them, depending on their age and their backgrounds. Mr. Pisces is full of romantic talk and sentimental poetry, while Miss Sagittarius is into athletic endeavors and philosophical debates. He interprets the world emotionally, while she interprets it as an intellectual challenge. He can sit perfectly still and experience a thousand moods, while she would rather experience a thousand zip codes and worry about her mood later. Yet despite their differences, they share a lot. They're both imaginative, flexible, dreamy people motivated by high ideals. They share less flattering characteristics as well: both can be a bit impractical, unreliable, and self-absorbed. Sexually, their imaginative approach makes them compatible, but when it comes to day-to-day reality, each of them may not quite provide what the other needs. Deep friendship may be the best idea for these two philosophers to contemplate.

He can be an intellectual rogue like Sagittarians
Kiefer Sutherland and John Malkovich, or a sexy
bad boy, like Archer men Brad Pitt and Judd Nelson.
He has a lust for life—and women—and needs a
mate who won't tie him down with too many commitments.
The right woman for him is smart and independent,
but spiritual and fun-loving, with
a sense of adventure that matches his own.

Sagittarius Man & Aries Woman

Ted Nugent seeks Chaka Khan.

This pair of adventure seekers lives for challenges, and dating each other may be their biggest surprise yet. If there's one woman who can get the zodiac's gypsy to stay put long enough to fall in love, it's Miss Aries. They'll rush the field at sports matches, go to midnight movies, and downhill ski at dawn on the first date. He's never had so much fun in one zip code—or in the bedroom, where this woman's athletic sex drive matches his. While she will maintain her own life even in a new relationship, she will make time to go on adventures with him, too. Since he's an eternal teacher and she's a precocious student, they enjoy learning new things together. What Mr. Sagittarius will discover as this relationship progresses is that things work well when he signs a long-term lease on love and lets Miss Aries drive the tour bus. As long as he's happy to let the sexy Ram navigate, this duo will enjoy life's challenges and appreciate the thrill of the journey.

Sagittarius Man & Taurus Woman

Randy Newman seeks Barbra Streisand.

The rambling Sagittarius man may find well-grounded Miss Taurus an unlikely partner for the adventure of romance, yet their opposing qualities broaden both of their perspectives on life. She is a stickler for stability and insists she needs a man with a steady career and paycheck. He insists on keeping his options open, and wants a mate to approve when he changes direction, residences, and priorities on a moment's notice. With compromise, self-reflection, and hard work, this duo can strike a balance between his need for variety and her need for stability. Their shared sense of humor will have them laughing all the way to the bedroom—where they make a lusty match—and can also help them gain perspective on their partnership. They connect on a deep level, because she teaches him the benefits of serious commitment. For his part, he teaches her that life is a series of constant changes, and that no amount of planning or routine will truly create the security she craves. If she accepts this lesson, their relationship will travel in the right direction, toward a life of lasting good humor.

Sagittarius Man & Gemini Woman

Jimi Hendrix seeks Lauryn Hill.

When the zodiac's two perpetual students enroll in Romance 101, they'll ace all the tests. Unlike other women Mr. Sagittarius has dated, outgoing Miss Gemini is game for any adventure, and right away he will sense he has met his soulmate. She loves to learn as much as he loves to travel, and because neither likes to waste precious time planning, they'll be off on adventures in no time. These two inspire each other. She has a way of getting him to think about what he's doing, while he can prompt her to pursue and achieve her dreams. In bed, she is his dream come true. Sexy, experimental Miss Gemini will try anything Mr. Sagittarius desires. Neither one of them likes to stay in one place for long, so if they marry they will enjoy far-flung travels. These like-minded people fulfill each other, and, together, find a life of wisdom and wild adventure.

Sagittarius Man & Cancer Woman

Little Richard seeks Debbie Harry.

♀   ♂

Domestic Miss Cancer and worldly Mr. Sagittarius have completely different ideas about home. Her motto could be "Home is where the hearth is," while his is "Wherever you go, there you are." Despite these differences, these two will see sparks at once. He finds this fragile woman creative, empathetic, and easy to talk to. She is attracted to his boyish optimism, although eventually she will demand a grown-up commitment. If he wants to capture her heart, he will have to eschew his incessant wanderlust and give domestic life with her a try. This sexy woman knows all sorts of ways to keep them entertained should he choose to unpack his bags—especially in the bedroom, where his energy is a good match for her sensual, patient approach. It won't always be easy. However, if Miss Cancer allows romance to override pragmatism and chooses him as a mate, he could teach her to be at home in the world rather than just at home by the fire. If Mr. Sagittarius allows her to tame him a bit, he'll find the ultimate journey—true love—right by Miss Cancer's side.

Sagittarius Man & Leo Woman

Ozzy Osbourne seeks Jennifer Lopez.

If she's the zodiac's diva, then he's the zodiac's roadie. He thinks she's funny and spirited, and she likes improvising as much as he does. He also appreciates the way Miss Leo shamelessly struts her stuff, and he doesn't mind playing the devoted fan. She likes his sense of adventure—this fiery woman wants a mate who will take her on a thrilling ride—and Mr. Sagittarius will take her to physical and spiritual places she's never been. Miss Leo makes a lot of demands and likes immediate gratification, but she's also generous and accepts the fact that Mr. Sagittarius sees life as a journey. She'll encourage him to take risks, unlike some women who want to rein him in and keep him nearer to home. He's not as luxury-oriented as she is, but knows how to provide the romance she needs. Their physical attraction will remain strong over time, as will the friendship that serves as a foundation for their relationship. There will be many loving scenes in this drama—and enough encores to last a lifetime.

Sagittarius Man & Virgo Woman

Dave Brubeck seeks Patsy Cline.

♀   ♂

This friendly pair is popular with others, but may not make the best company when alone. Miss Virgo is terrified of needless risk, and the Sagittarian man is terrified of needless monotony. They both have only the best intentions, but this duo is not a match made in heaven. Sweet Miss Virgo won't understand his boyish jokes, and Mr. Sagittarius will have a hard time taking her earnest love of order and organization seriously. They'll offend each other without meaning to, and while their opposite personalities can seem comically at odds to their friends, who will find their efforts at romance endearing, it won't take them long to realize that the differences outweigh their shared strengths. In the bedroom, her modesty frustrates him, while his enthusiasm makes her nervous. As a long-distance relationship, this has possibilities, since both of these signs need independence. A life of matrimony is less likely—unless he decides he wants a partner to shape his free-form lifestyle and she decides to embrace the chaos he adores.

Sagittarius Man & Libra Woman

Billy Idol seeks Tiffany.

This duo is among the most cheerful and charismatic in the zodiac. Miss Libra is attractive, polite, and persuasive—and Mr. Sagittarius adores her polished sociability, because it means he can take her everywhere. She is willing to follow wherever this sexy, masculine man leads, and his daredevil side excites her. These signs communicate well together and will ease into love successfully. They also spur each other toward better decision-making, since they can convince themselves—and other people—that anything is possible. She thinks carefully about her choices, while he acts before thinking. Her witty conversation and his adventurous lifestyle will always keep the pace lively. In the bedroom, it's all sparks and plenty of long-lasting flames for these two. She's breathy and seductive, while he's athletic and experimental, and they intuitively know how to take turns leading and following. Miss Libra may be one of the few women who can get this playboy to settle down—although for these two, monogamy will never mean monotony.

Sagittarius Man & Scorpio Woman

Frank Zappa seeks Bjork.

♀ ♂

Miss Scorpio and Mr. Sagittarius are two of the zodiac's sexiest signs, and they share a love of philosophy. This highly charged duo can talk—and make passionate love—for hours. Both signs are also daring, but her sense of adventure is far different from his. While she's open to change, especially as it affects her personal growth, each time she slides into a new incarnation of herself she brings a bit of the past with her. He appreciates this depth, but ultimately may wish she could experience change more casually, as he does, without so much emotional baggage. Since she's more discriminating about friends and money than he is, Mr. Sagittarius will also question her open-mindedness. In the end, he may feel Miss Scorpio is too serious to understand his exuberant experience of life. Meanwhile, she may feel he's experiencing the Cliff's Notes version of spiritual travels that affect her deeply. However, what they learn by working to combat their incompatibilities may surprise them. She could learn to travel more lightly, while he could learn to empathize more deeply with the world.

Sagittarius Man & Sagittarius Woman

Chuck Mangione seeks Dionne Warwick.

These two will befriend one another first. Once a connection begins, it can't help but grow into romance. He loves the way good-humored Miss Sagittarius is ready for any new adventure, and she's delighted that he supports her independent lifestyle. She encourages him to try out his dreams, and he supports her sporting interests. Now and then they'll snap at each other, usually when they've tired themselves out from too much adventure, but this blunt duo forgives and forgets easily. Sexually, they share a similar athletic approach that is comfortable for both of them, but they will have to experiment to keep the variety alive. While this pair is friendly and sociable, the more time they spend together, the less time they may make for others, as they don't like the way a constant crowd cramps their style. They'll have to remind themselves that other people help spice up the evening rather than reduce its possibilities. They'll never lack for great company, since everyone wants to be around this dynamic duo.

Sagittarius Man & Capricorn Woman

Bruce Hornsby seeks Crystal Gayle.

♀ ♂

This relationship begins with great enthusiasm, but might flicker out when the initial sexual sparks die down. Mr. Sagittarius likes her ambition, drive, and feminine way of wielding power over every situation. Miss Capricorn likes the way he follows his gut instincts without getting hung up on what other people think. They both put considerable amounts of time into continuing their education throughout their lives, but while he pursues far-flung travel or spiritual growth, she hones skills that deepen her professional competency. She likes stability, tradition, and hard work, and wants to finish the things she begins—and she's not so sure a relationship with an Archer will last. He is deeply attracted to her, but in the bedroom they may not be able to connect on the emotional level she needs. Sexual sparks aside, this duo will have to work to create an environment where he feels free to travel and she feels confident he's coming home. This might work best as a casual relationship—for a successful commitment, these two stubborn people must be willing to compromise.

Sagittarius Man & Aquarius Woman

Sammy Davis Jr. seeks Roberta Flack.

There's no question that this is a winning duo. The independent, boyish Archer and sociable Aquarian woman make an excellent match. When he says with a poker face that he just took a trip to the mythical underwater land of Atlantis, she'll give him a wink and ask to see the pictures and what the natives were like. In addition to their shared sense of humor, these two have big hearts; he won't mind if she's donating their tax refund for world peace or running a homeless shelter in the guest wing. In bed, she's eccentric and open-minded, and will try anything he suggests. She curbs his blunt manner with her friendly one, while he's direct enough to pull her away from her perpetual crowd of friends when he senses she needs a break. They'll be the life of any party they attend—and they'll attend every party they're invited to. There's never a dull moment for this unstoppable pair.

Sagittarius Man & Pisces Woman

Lou Rawls seeks Nina Simone.

These two have many traits in common, but the sort of stability that a love relationship requires isn't one of them. Miss Pisces is sexy, sensitive, and imaginative, but her emotions often throw her into a passive funk Mr. Sagittarius can't understand. She finds him inspiring and optimistic, but his blunt comments often hurt her feelings and his tendency to change plans confuses her. Sexually, they are imaginative lovers and know how to fulfill each other's fantasies. However, reality for this pair can be difficult. She travels in her fantasy life, where her response to the environment around her stirs daydreams and creativity. His version of travel is literal, and nothing broadens the horizons or inspires a Sagittarian more than visiting a faraway place. She instead needs someone who can unearth her mysterious emotions and respond to them, not take them on the road. What he needs is someone who will thrive in the new environments he's always seeking. They can appreciate each other deeply, but their most fruitful union may be as friends.

The Sagittarian home is filled with treasures from far-flung travels and will be decorated with art and artifacts unearthed in unusual places. Since those born under this sign love animals and the outdoors, their décor may resemble a cross between a natural history museum and a hunting lodge. They favor wood-paneled walls and art depicting the wilderness. Sagittarians can live well in small spaces, and life in a city often appeals to them—impulsive Archers want speedy access to friends, work, night life, and culture. Less urban individuals of this sporting sign might prefer a big but informal country house with lots of land. While these on-the-go folks may have only a few children, they almost always have lots of pets. Archers love dogs in particular, and will lovingly decorate a doghouse or shop for gourmet canine treats. Many Sagittarians, unable to decide if, when, or where to settle down, will be long-term renters—preferably with several apartments in major cities around the globe.

The Sagittarian body tends to be tall and leggy, and natives of this sign tend to stay slender because they remain on the go throughout the day. Their optimistic outlook and love of sports keeps them in shape, but they are also more prone than those of other signs toward sports injuries. This sign rules the hips and thighs, and Sagittarians need to take extra care to stretch these parts of the body and walk often to keep them in good condition. Sagittarius also rules the liver, which means a high-fat diet and too much alcohol can lead to strain. Those born under the sign of the Archer sometimes overestimate their own fitness and should be patient enough to stretch and warm up before enthusiastically trying any new sport. This overenthusiasm can also apply to their habit of staying up late. Active Sagittarians should consider eating several mini-meals throughout the day to keep their energy levels consistent. Generally, these fortunate people have a positive mental outlook that keeps them healthy well into their golden years.

Sagittarians prefer casual dress, and pepper their wardrobe with unusual finds that they discover during their travel. This sign's look is somewhat collegiate: Archers gravitate toward comfortable clothes they can wear all day long, since they never know in the morning what their day might hold. Sagittarians shop with their signature enthusiasm, diving into crowded stores and plundering racks for buried treasure. They don't covet or obsess over material things; they either buy what they want right away or forget about it. These adventurers can get away with some outrageous outfits, but Sagittarians are more likely to spend money on sporty looks than formal dresses. High-tech all-condition jackets and top-notch hiking boots are the kinds of items destined for the Archer wardrobe. This sign's best color is purple, a royal and religious color that signifies the Sagittarian philosophical streak, and its stone is turquoise.

Sagittarians are natural travelers who enjoy traveling alone as well as in a group. Because they want to cover as much distance as possible, they love to visit foreign countries and have no trouble roughing it in one-star hotels or youth hostels if their budget doesn't allow for finer digs. The point of travel, for a Sagittarius, is to expand the mind. The longer the trip, the better; rather than get homesick, Sagittarians are likely to prolong a journey. Adventurous and athletic, they like to visit places few people can reach, and enjoy trekking through Alaska, navigating a remote river, or climbing a volcano. They also like spiritual exploration, and visiting holy sites, taking religious retreats, or traveling to far-flung meditation centers, all of which satisfy the Sagittarian desire for inner growth.

Those born under this sign like casual entertaining and love to introduce guests to cuisines from faraway places. Whether Archers throw a party in an Ethiopian restaurant where all the guests eat with their fingers or suggest a Korean barbecue place where coals burn under the table, the Sagittarian dinner party will be an adventure. These folks also love outdoor entertaining, from picnics near lakes and mountains to tailgate parties at sporting events. Sagittarians like spicy food, and will be well-versed in the culinary traditions of the many cultures they've explored. While impatient Archers are more likely to call up a nearby restaurant than try cooking Indian or Thai at home, now and then they will pull off an excellent and creative dinner party. These folks will throw a tea and tarot card reading party complete with British high tea, or serve great jambalaya during Mardi Gras week. Whatever the occasion, Sagittarians will see to it that guests try another world cuisine before they go home.

In the Company of Sagittarius

Musicians:
Christina Aguilera
Noel Coward
Sammy Davis Jr.
Sheila E.
Connie Francis
Ira Gershwin
Robert Goulet
Amy Grant
Jimi Hendrix
Billy Idol
Etta Jones
Scott Joplin
Stacy Lattisaw
Brenda Lee
Jim Morrison (Doors)
Randy Newman
Ted Nugent
Sinead O'Connor
Ozzy Osbourne
Donny Osmond
Edith Piaf
June Pointer
　(Pointer Sisters)
Lou Rawls
Little Richard
Dawn Robinson
　(En Vogue)

Britney Spears
Tina Turner
Dionne Warwick
Frank Zappa

Performers:
Woody Allen
Kim Basinger
Kenneth Branagh
Beau Bridges
Judi Dench
Phil Donahue
Kirk Douglas
Jane Fonda
Teri Garr
Betty Grable
Daryl Hannah
Bruce Lee
Lucy Liu
John Malkovich
Harpo Marx
Bette Midler
Ricardo Montalban
Julianne Moore
Judd Nelson
Brad Pitt
Christopher Plummer
Kiefer Sutherland
Cicely Tyson
Dick Van Dyke
Flip Wilson

Reformers:
Winston Churchill
Charles De Gaulle
Benjamin Disraeli
Jean Paul Getty
Fiorello La Guardia
Claude Lévi-Strauss
Nostradamus

Artists:
Wassily Kandinsky
Paul Klee
Edward Munch
Jose Orozco
Diego Rivera
Charles Schulz
Georges Seurat
Steven Spielberg
Henri de Toulouse-Lautrec
William Wegman

Athletes:
Boris Becker
Larry Bird
Ty Cobb
Joe DiMaggio
Bo Jackson
Florence Griffith Joyner
Billie Jean King
Cathy Rigby
Monica Seles
Katarina Witt

Writers:
James Agee
Louisa May Alcott
Jane Austen
William Blake
T. Coraghessan Boyle
Rita Mae Brown
William F. Buckley Jr.
Erskine Caldwell
Willa Cather
Joseph Conrad
Emily Dickinson
George Eliot
Penelope Fitzgerald
Gustave Flaubert
Heinrich Heine
Eugene Ionesco
Shirley Jackson
C. S. Lewis
Sue Miller
Patrick O'Brian
Rainer Maria Rilke
Muriel Rukeyser
William Safire
Saki
Aleksandr Solzhenitsyn
James Thurber
Mark Twain
Rebecca West

Permissions

Don't Worry, Be Happy
Bobby McFerrin
(Bobby McFerrin)
℗ 1988 Capitol Records, Inc., under license from
EMI-Capitol Music Special Markets.

I'm So Excited
Pointer Sisters
(Anita Pointer/June Pointer/Ruth Pointer/
Trevor Lawrence)
℗ 1982 Planet Records, under license from
BMG Direct Marketing, Inc.

All Fired Up
Pat Benatar
(Kerryn Tolhurst/Pat Benatar)
℗ 1988 Chrysalis Records Inc., under license from
EMI-Capitol Music Special Markets.

All Right Now
Free
(Andy Fraser/Paul Rodgers)
Courtesy of Universal Music Enterprises, a Division
of UMG Recordings, Inc.

Ramblin' Man
The Allman Brothers Band
(Dickey Betts)
℗ 1973 Capricorn Records, courtesy of Universal Music
Enterprises, a Division of UMG Recordings, Inc.

One Tin Soldier (The Legend of Billy Jack)
Coven
(Dennis Lambert/Brian Potter)
Produced under license from Warner Bros. Records Inc.

Share the Land
The Guess Who
(Burton Cummings)
Courtesy of the RCA Records Label.

Last Train to Clarksville
The Monkees
(Tommy Boyce/Bobby Hart)
Controlled by Rhino Entertainment Company.

The Happy Song (Dum-Dum)
Otis Redding
(Otis Redding/Steve Cropper)
Produced under license from Atlantic Recording Corp.

Everyday
Buddy Holly
(Charles Hardin/Norman Petty)
Courtesy of Universal Music Special Markets, Inc.

Truth and Honesty
Aretha Franklin
(Peter Allen/Burt Bacharach/Carole Bayer Sayer)
℗ 1981 Arista Records, Inc., under license from BMG Special Products.

Sagittarius
Cannonball Adderley featuring The Nat Adderley Sextet
(Roy McCurdy/Rick Holmes)
℗ 1972 Capitol Records, Inc., under license from EMI-Capitol
Music Special Markets.

This Compilation ℗ 2001 Rhino Entertainment Company.